DEFENDING THE CHURCH AGAINST THE PAGAN THREAT

Lucas Miles Unmasks Paganism and Godless Uprising Corrupting Christians Faith and Liberty

ALEX WEST

Disclaimer
This book is intended to inform and encourage readers in their spiritual journey and understanding of the challenges facing the Church today. The ideas and opinions expressed in this book are those of the author and do not necessarily reflect the views of any organization, group, or individual with whom the author is affiliated.

While every effort has been made to provide accurate and up-to-date information, the author and publisher make no representations or warranties with respect to the completeness, accuracy, or reliability of the contents, and any reliance you place on such information is at your own risk.

This book is an independent work and is not affiliated with Lucas Miles or any of his publications unless explicitly stated. Any references to Lucas Miles's work are provided for the purpose of context and commentary, and all quotations and references are used in compliance with fair use.

The contents of this book are for informational purposes only and are not intended as legal, medical, or professional advice. The author encourages readers to seek the counsel of appropriate professionals in specific matters.

Table of Contents

Dedication

To those who stand firm in faith,
to the defenders of truth,
and to those who courageously rise against the
godless uprising.
May this work equip you to boldly defend the
Church and preserve liberty for future
generations.

Acknowledgments

First and foremost, I want to express my deepest gratitude to God for His guidance, wisdom, and unwavering strength throughout the writing of this book. Without His inspiration, this work would not have come to life.

I also owe a heartfelt thanks to my family, whose constant support, encouragement, and patience provided the foundation for this project. To my dear friends and mentors, thank you for your insight, prayers, and encouragement during the writing process.

A special thank you to Lucas Miles for his thought-provoking work, which has served as a catalyst for much of this book. His courage in confronting today's spiritual and cultural challenges has inspired many, including myself, to take action.

Lastly, thank you to my readers and those who seek to understand and engage with the truth. Your dedication to God and His Word fuels the mission to stand strong against the rising tide of paganism.

Preface

In today's rapidly changing world, the Church faces an unprecedented challenge. Across the globe, Christianity is under attack,not through direct persecution alone, but through a growing cultural shift that seeks to undermine the very foundation of our faith. This is not merely a battle against secular ideologies, but a spiritual battle against the resurgence of ancient pagan beliefs, now repackaged and woven into the fabric of modern society.

The **Pagan Threat** is real, and it's here, in the form of cultural ideologies and movements that are slowly, yet steadily, eroding the values and truths that the Church has stood upon for centuries. From the rise of woke culture and techno-paganism to the subtle but dangerous allure of radical inclusivity, the pagan revival is gaining ground in ways we may not even fully recognize. These forces have infiltrated the media, politics, education, and even the Church itself, making it essential for believers to understand the threat and respond accordingly.

This book is not merely a warning, but a call to action. We, as the Church, cannot sit idly by while our faith and freedom are slowly eroded by ideologies that distort the truth of the Gospel. Now more than ever, we must defend the sacred truths handed down to us and stand firm in the face of an ever-encroaching darkness.

Defending the Church Against the Pagan Threat is my response to this cultural and spiritual crisis. It is an exploration of the pagan ideologies that threaten our faith, a roadmap for how the Church can rise to the occasion, and a practical guide for Christians to not only withstand this threat but to actively reclaim the public square for Christ.

I believe that the Church can and must stand strong in the face of these challenges. But this requires more than just passive resistance. It demands a reawakening of faith, a deep commitment to biblical truth, and a revival that empowers Christians to engage the culture boldly and effectively.

The journey you are about to embark on in these pages is not just about identifying the threats we face—it's about equipping you, the believer, to take action. In these pages, you will find practical strategies to strengthen your faith, empower your spiritual leadership, and engage effectively in the public arena. Above all, you will discover how to reclaim the narrative, pushing back against the forces that seek to undermine God's truth and preserving His Kingdom on earth.

I urge you, as you read this book, to consider your role in the fight ahead. The future of the Church and our freedoms depend on the boldness and commitment of believers like you. Together, we can and will defend the faith, fortify our communities, and ultimately ensure that the light of Christ continues to shine brightly in the face of a godless uprising.

Introduction: Understanding the Pagan Threat Facing the Church

The world we live in today is unlike anything we've seen in recent history. Christianity, once central to much of the West, now faces a cultural tide that seeks to weaken its influence and challenge its core truths. The threat we face is not one of overt persecution, but something more subtle—a cultural shift that is quietly undermining the foundation of Christian beliefs and values. This is the Pagan Threat, a growing force reshaping our world in ways many Christians have yet to fully comprehend.

The pagan revival we're witnessing today is not merely a return to ancient belief systems, although we can see traces of these ideas. It's a threat that takes shape through modern ideologies—secular movements that have embedded themselves deeply in education, politics, entertainment, and even parts of the Church. From woke culture to techno paganism, these ideologies distort the truth, challenge morality, and aim to replace traditional Christian values with new, often contradictory, beliefs.

But this issue goes beyond just ideology. It strikes at the very soul of the Church, at the heart of the faith, and at the future of freedom. These forces are not neutral; they seek to replace the very truths that have guided Christianity for centuries. The Church **(the body of Christ)** is being called to rise up and defend what it has always stood for, from its message to its mission.

This book is not just about recognizing the threats facing the Church. It is a call to action. It will help you understand the cultural and spiritual forces that are currently working to distort and destroy Christianity. It is also a guide on how to stand firm in your faith, how to resist these forces, and how to help safeguard the next generation from the false ideologies gaining strength today.

As you read, you will learn about the nature of the pagan threat, how it has evolved, and why it's especially dangerous today. You will discover practical steps to fortify your faith, defend against the falsehoods being spread through our culture, and protect your family and community from these modern-day idols.

This is not a time to remain passive. The battle for faith, truth, and liberty is already underway. The question is not if this battle will happen, but whether we, as Christians, will be ready to fight. The battle is happening now, and we must rise to meet it, prepared to defend our faith and our freedom.

As you read, I hope you will not only gain clarity on these challenges but also feel empowered to take action. By the end of this book, I trust you will be ready to stand strong, equipped to defend the faith, and prepared to confront the pagan threats of our time.

Chapter 1: The Resurgence of Pagan Ideologies

In the early days of Christianity, the Church faced a direct and overt threat from the surrounding pagan cultures—religions that promoted the worship of multiple gods, human self-interest, and rituals that were directly opposed to Christian teachings. Today, while the physical temples and idols may be gone, we are witnessing a resurgence of these ancient ideologies, not in the form of rituals or idols but through contemporary secular movements that echo the spiritual and moral themes of paganism. These movements, which have embedded themselves deeply in our cultural fabric, seek to replace Christian values with new, self-centered belief systems that can fundamentally undermine the Christian faith.

Wokeism: The New Moral Authority

One of the most prominent movements we see today is wokeism. On the surface, it appears to champion justice, equality, and the fight against oppression. These ideals, at first glance, align with Christian values of love, justice, and compassion. However, the deeper we look, the more we see how wokeism, despite its appearance, mirrors certain aspects of ancient paganism—particularly in its emphasis on individual autonomy, moral relativism, and collective moral authority.

In traditional Christian doctrine, truth is seen as absolute, grounded in the unchanging nature of God. Christianity teaches that God's law is the standard of morality and that each person, regardless of race, gender, or socioeconomic status, is equal in His eyes. In contrast, wokeism asserts that morality is fluid and subjective—defined by societal constructs that can shift with the times. This is similar to the pagan belief systems, where what was considered right or wrong often depended on the whims of various gods or the prevailing cultural norms. In pagan cultures, there was no consistent moral framework—morality was dictated by whatever was in favor at the moment, and it shifted depending on the needs of society or the political elite.

For instance, in recent years, debates about gender identity and pronouns have become one of the most visible aspects of wokeism. While Christianity teaches that God created mankind in His image as male and female, wokeism asserts that gender is a social construct and can be chosen based on personal identity. This challenges the Christian belief in the sanctity of God's design for human nature. The normalization of multiple gender identities is akin to the pagan practice of elevating human will above divine order, allowing personal desires to redefine reality.

Moreover, wokeism's approach to justice—rooted in identity politics—often emphasizes group identity over individual moral accountability. This focus on collective group rights, often at the expense of personal responsibility or objective moral standards, parallels the pagan worldview where social order was maintained not by adherence to universal truth, but by appeasing the whims of powerful entities or social groups.

Techno-Paganism: The Deification of Technology

Another growing movement that reflects pagan themes is techno-paganism, the increasing reverence for technology as a force that can transcend human limitations. In ancient pagan societies, gods and spirits were believed to possess extraordinary powers, capable of manipulating the natural world in ways that humans could not. Similarly, modern techno-paganism elevates technology to a godlike status, where it is seen as the key to solving humanity's greatest problems—curing diseases, extending life, and even transcending death itself.

The rise of transhumanism, for example, which aims to enhance human capabilities through technology—whether through genetic modifications, artificial intelligence, or brain-computer interfaces—parallels the ancient pagan belief that humanity could control nature and reshape existence through divine-like power. Just as pagans once sought to manipulate the natural world and influence their gods to achieve prosperity, modern techno-paganism seeks to harness technology to achieve immortality, create perfect societies, and elevate human existence above natural limitations.

Consider the growing fascination with artificial intelligence and digital avatars. The belief that AI could one day surpass human intelligence and lead us to a new phase of existence echoes the pagan aspiration to tap into a higher power or ultimate knowledge. Techno-paganism views technology not merely as a tool, but as a deity capable of bringing about salvation or a new form of human existence. This undermines the Christian worldview, which teaches that true salvation and transformation come only through Christ, not human-made creations.

Identity Politics: A New Form of Idolatry

Identity politics, too, has grown in prominence and presents a modern form of idolatry—one that mirrors the polytheistic tendencies of ancient paganism. Just as pagan societies worshipped multiple gods, each representing a different aspect of life or human desire, identity politics elevates various aspects of individual identity—race, gender, sexual orientation—into the highest form of moral authority. In this worldview, one's identity is not just a personal characteristic but the defining feature that determines moral worth, social status, and rights.

Christianity, on the other hand, teaches that all people are made in the image of God, regardless of their identity markers, and that true moral worth comes from being a child of God, not from what labels society places on an individual. Christianity calls us to see one another through the lens of God's love and grace, offering forgiveness and transformation, not based on our identity, but on Christ's work.

But in identity politics, identity becomes the new "idol." Personal identity markers are placed on a pedestal, often above the unchanging truths of God's Word. This leads to the worship of self rather than the Creator. The focus shifts from biblical morality—what is just, pure, and holy—to a more fragmented moral system that changes according to each identity's needs. As in ancient paganism, where individuals or communities would align themselves with specific deities based on their desires or struggles, identity politics places individuals in opposing tribes, where loyalty to one's identity group becomes the primary moral compass, often at the cost of unity and mutual respect.

Modern Secularism: The New Humanism

Secularism and humanism also reflect aspects of paganism, particularly in their rejection of divine authority and embrace of human autonomy. In secular humanism, human reason and intellect are elevated above divine revelation. This mirrors the ancient pagan belief in human agency—where humans sought to control their own fate without the need for divine intervention.

Today, secular humanism promotes the idea that humanity has the power to determine what is right and wrong, often discarding the moral guidelines set forth in Scripture. This view rejects the need for divine authority, which is central to Christianity. Instead, it promotes a relativistic worldview where morality is subjective and dependent on individual or collective choice.

This rejection of absolute truth—the belief that there is no higher authority than human reason—echoes ancient pagan thought, where each city-state had its own gods and moral framework, constantly shifting depending on the needs or will of the people. Christianity, however, holds that there is one true God, whose moral order is eternal and unchanging.

In sum, while modern secular ideologies like wokeism, techno-paganism, and identity politics may appear progressive or liberating on the surface, they are deeply rooted in ancient paganism. They share a common thread: the elevation of human autonomy and self-worship, at the expense of divine truth and order. These movements challenge the core tenets of Christianity, which teaches that truth is absolute, rooted in God, and that human dignity and morality come from being

made in God's image, not from the
ever-shifting sands of societal constructs.

As Christians, we must recognize these
ideological threats not just as abstract
social movements but as spiritual
challenges that seek to erode the very
foundations of our faith. By understanding
the historical and ideological roots of these
movements, we can better prepare to
defend our faith against them, standing
firm in the truth of God's Word and the
enduring wisdom it offers for all
generations.

Chapter 2: The Church's Role in Confronting the Pagan Uprising

As the pagan ideologies continue to gain ground in modern culture, the Church finds itself at a critical juncture. The battle is not just ideological; it is spiritual. The Church's role in confronting the pagan uprising is both a sacred duty and an urgent mission. The Church is called not only to preserve the gospel but to actively engage with the culture that is increasingly hostile to its message. This chapter will explore the biblical mandate for the Church to stand firm, the vital role of spiritual leadership, and the practical ways the Church can confront these ideologies with courage and clarity.

The Biblical Mandate: Stand Firm in the Faith

The Church has a clear and unequivocal mandate from Scripture to stand firm in the face of false ideologies. The apostle Paul's instruction to the Ephesians, "Put on the full armor of God" (Ephesians 6:10-18), speaks directly to the need for vigilance and spiritual readiness in times of cultural and ideological upheaval. Just as the early Church faced persecution from pagan ideologies, so too does the Church today face a wave of secular and idolatrous ideas that challenge the very foundation of Christian belief.

It is easy for the Church to retreat into a defensive position, hoping the world's changes will pass. However, the Bible makes it clear that passivity is not an option. The Apostle Paul writes in 1 Corinthians 16:13, "Be on your guard; stand firm in the faith; be courageous; be strong." The Church is called to be a beacon of truth, a firm and unyielding presence in a world that is quickly redefining morality, purpose, and even human nature.

The challenge today is not just the presence of these pagan ideologies but their pervasiveness and influence. These ideas infiltrate education, media, politics, and even religious institutions. The rise of secular humanism, wokeism, techno-paganism, and identity politics requires the Church to take action, not only by holding firmly to Scripture but by actively engaging in the cultural conversations of our time.

The Role of Spiritual Leadership

In facing this cultural and spiritual crisis, the Church's leadership is crucial. Spiritual leaders—pastors, teachers, and church leaders—are tasked with guiding the flock through this turbulent time. However, leadership is not simply about teaching doctrine; it is about modeling it. The Church's leaders must embody the biblical principles they preach, providing both wisdom and strength as the congregation faces these challenges.

Spiritual leadership requires courage. It's easy to preach about standing firm in the face of persecution when it's hypothetical, but when the battle is real—when the congregation faces pressure to conform to secular beliefs—true leaders will take a stand. This involves more than just teaching from the pulpit. It requires pastors to engage the culture directly, providing answers to the questions being posed by society, and giving their congregation the tools to do the same.

For instance, when discussing issues like the redefinition of gender, spiritual leaders can model how to address such topics with biblical truth, compassion, and clarity. This is not just about opposing an idea—it's about showing how the truth of Scripture applies to contemporary issues in a way that is both firm and loving.

Engaging Culture: Practical Steps for the Church

The Church cannot afford to remain on the sidelines. Cultural engagement is not a secondary task; it is central to the Church's mission. The Great Commission (Matthew 28:19-20) calls the Church to go out into the world, making disciples of all nations. This means that the Church must actively engage with the world in order to fulfill its calling. It's not enough to teach doctrine in isolation; the Church must equip its people to bring that doctrine to life in every area of society.

1. Teach Biblical Truth with Clarity and Boldness

The foundation of cultural engagement begins with teaching. If Christians are to defend their faith against pagan ideologies, they must first be deeply rooted in Scripture. This means teaching not just the **"what"** but also the **"why"** behind Christian beliefs. In a world that often challenges biblical morality, a clear and solid understanding of Scripture is essential. Leaders must teach their congregations to not only know the Bible but to understand it in a way that equips them to navigate the moral and cultural issues of today.

2. Empower Believers to Defend Their Faith

The Church is a community, and every believer has a role to play in defending the faith. It is not enough for the pastor to stand firm; the entire congregation must be prepared to do the same. Apologetics, the practice of defending the faith with reasoned arguments, is essential in today's world. Pastors should teach their congregations how to address challenges to the Christian faith, whether it's questions about the existence of God, moral issues, or questions about the Bible's authority.

The Church must equip believers with the ability to articulate their faith and respond to the false ideologies they encounter in the world. Whether it's engaging in a discussion about morality, gender, or the value of human life, Christians must be ready to speak with both truth and love.

3. Build a Culture of Discipleship

Discipleship is the process by which the Church strengthens its members in their faith, helping them grow spiritually so they can stand firm in the face of opposition. Discipleship programs should focus on more than just knowledge—they should also focus on transformation. The Church should not only teach doctrine but also model how to live out that doctrine in the world.

As we see more secular and pagan ideas infiltrate the culture, the need for biblical discipleship becomes more pressing. A strong discipleship program can help young believers form a firm foundation in their faith before they are exposed to ideologies that challenge biblical truth. Discipleship should teach Christians to think biblically about culture, politics, and social issues, so they are not easily swayed by the world's views.

4. Engage in Spiritual Warfare Through Prayer and Action

Spiritual warfare is real, and it is essential for the Church to engage in it. Ephesians 6:12 reminds us that our struggle is not against flesh and blood but against the spiritual forces of evil in the heavenly realms. Prayer is one of the most powerful tools in the believer's arsenal. The Church must engage in prayer, not just for personal needs but for the defense of the faith and the salvation of those caught in false ideologies.

Additionally, the Church must take action. Prayer should lead to concrete steps—whether it's advocating for religious freedom, supporting biblical values in the public sphere, or providing practical help to those affected by secular ideologies.

5. Support Christian Organizations that Defend the Faith

While individual churches can do a lot, the larger Church body also has a role to play. There are numerous Christian organizations that are on the front lines, defending religious liberty, advocating for Christian values in politics, and promoting biblical education. Churches should actively support these organizations, whether through financial contributions, volunteer work, or prayer. By partnering with organizations that defend the faith in the public square, the Church can amplify its impact.

Spiritual Leadership: A Call for Courage and Integrity

Spiritual leadership is the backbone of the Church's response to the pagan uprising. Leaders are tasked not only with teaching but also with modeling the strength and integrity needed to stand firm in the faith. It's important for leaders to be vocal about the issues of our time, not only in theological terms but in practical, everyday terms. By leading with clarity, courage, and consistency, spiritual leaders can inspire their congregations to rise to the challenge.

Furthermore, leaders must be willing to take risks. In today's climate, standing firm for biblical truth may come at a cost. But as Jesus said in Matthew 16:18, "The gates of hell will not prevail against it." The Church's leadership must trust that, no matter the opposition, God's truth will always triumph in the end.

The Church's role in confronting the pagan uprising is clear: it must stand firm in faith, teach biblical truth boldly, and actively engage with the culture. Spiritual leaders are the ones who will guide the Church through these turbulent times, and the strength of the Church will be determined by how well it equips its people to face the challenges ahead. By engaging in prayer, discipleship, cultural action, and support for Christian organizations, the Church can withstand the pagan ideologies of today and emerge stronger in the faith.

The battle is not just ideological; it is spiritual, and the Church must rise to meet it with courage, clarity, and unwavering commitment to the truth of God's Word.

Chapter 3: Key Ideologies Undermining the Faith

In a world increasingly marked by division and confusion, the Church faces profound challenges in holding fast to biblical truth. Today, several powerful ideologies are not only reshaping society but are actively undermining the faith itself. Among these, wokeism and techno-paganism stand out as two of the most pervasive threats to Christian doctrine and the moral foundation of Western society. These movements, while seemingly distinct, share roots in ancient pagan beliefs and challenge the core values of Christianity. In this chapter, we will explore how these ideologies function, their intersection with pagan thought, and their profound impact on society. We will also examine how identity politics fits into this framework, drawing parallels with ancient pagan practices.

Wokeism and Its Intersection with Pagan Thought

At its surface, wokeism claims to champion social justice, equality, and the fight against oppression. It emphasizes the importance of recognizing systemic racism, privilege, and inequality. On its face, these goals may seem aligned with Christian principles of justice and compassion. However, a deeper look reveals a troubling pattern: wokeism is more than just a social movement; it is a secular religion that seeks to replace traditional Christian moral structures with new, evolving ideologies that challenge biblical truth.

Lucas Miles, in his book *The Pagan Threat,* warns about the subtle way in which these modern movements, though claiming to fight for justice, are rooted in a worldview that mirrors ancient pagan belief systems. Wokeism embodies the same spirit of rebellion that marked the ancient pagan cultures, where individual autonomy was placed above divine law, and truth became subjective rather than absolute. In pagan societies, there was no clear, unchanging moral order. Morality was often based on the will of the gods, which could change depending on political or social needs. This mirrors how wokeism has evolved into a fluid moral framework, where what is considered just or right can shift to accommodate new cultural demands.

The intersection with paganism becomes evident when we consider the idolization of identity within woke culture. Just as ancient pagan societies worshipped a variety of gods and deities, modern society has replaced divinity with identity, making personal identity—whether through race, gender, or sexual orientation—the highest point of self-definition and moral authority. This is a shift away from traditional Christian values, where the image of God is seen as the defining characteristic of every person, not the ever-changing constructs of human identity.

Moreover, wokeism often demands loyalty and conformity, much like the ancient pagan cults. If you do not adhere to the moral code, you risk being labeled as an enemy of progress, much in the same way those who did not worship the pagan gods were ostracized or punished. This tribal mindset is deeply divisive, creating a culture where unity is sacrificed for ideological purity.

As wokeism continues to gain traction, particularly in America, its influence can be seen in the cultural uprising that Lucas Miles describes in The Pagan Threat. The godless uprising is not limited to the rise of secular atheism but is further fueled by the rise of movements like wokeism, which reject traditional biblical norms and substitute them with their own evolving set of beliefs. This shift is not only spiritually dangerous but has far-reaching implications for social cohesion and freedom.

The Rise of Techno-Paganism and the Idolization of Technology

One of the more insidious threats to Christianity today is the rise of techno-paganism—a belief system that blends modern technology with spiritual practices and ideologies. It is a manifestation of the worship of technology, where devices, platforms, and digital networks are revered almost as divine entities. This new form of paganism places human progress and technological innovation at the center of existence, elevating them to a status previously reserved for gods and spirits in ancient pagan cultures.

Techno-paganism is growing as technology becomes more integrated into every facet of human life. We see it in the rise of transhumanism, the belief that humanity can be transcended through technology—making us, in effect, more than human. From the pursuit of artificial intelligence that mimics the human mind to the use of digital avatars that promise to extend human life through virtual or augmented realities, technology is being deified. The promise of immortality and the ability to manipulate human biology in ways once reserved for gods are deeply spiritual promises that are attracting millions. These ideas offer a new religion, one that doesn't need a god, but instead, places its hope in scientific advancement and the mastery of nature.

Like ancient pagans, techno-pagans believe that human beings are masters of their own fate, no longer subject to the will of a higher power. Technology offers a way to reshape reality and create our own truth, much as ancient people sought to appease gods or manipulate nature for their own benefit. This worldview, however, strips humanity of its divine purpose and creates a hollow, idolatrous system that worships human ingenuity and control, rather than acknowledging a Creator who designed and sustains all things.

The spiritual implications of techno-paganism are profound. Instead of acknowledging a higher power [**God as the source of all wisdom and truth**] this ideology places human reason and technological power at the center of existence. As technology continues to advance, so does the temptation to worship the very tools and systems that were once created to serve humanity. This modern idolization of technology is more than just a cultural trend; it is a form of spiritual bondage that blinds people to the true source of life.

Identity Politics and Its Roots in Ancient Pagan Rituals and Beliefs

Identity politics is one of the most divisive movements in contemporary society. It places individual identity—whether based on race, gender, or sexual orientation—at the center of political and social life. While the call for equality and recognition of marginalized communities has its roots in legitimate social justice concerns, identity politics often devolves into a cult of self-worship.

The roots of identity politics can be traced back to ancient pagan beliefs, where the worship of personal identity or selfhood took precedence. In many ancient cultures, gods were seen as representations of human desires and needs—gods of fertility, power, wealth, or war. Similarly, identity politics has become a system of worshiping individual identity and placing it at the center of moral and societal value.

In the pagan world, these beliefs were often tied to rituals and practices that exalted individual identity, often through public ceremonies, sacrifices, and rites. Today, identity politics takes the form of social rituals, where personal identity is celebrated and affirmed as the highest moral and political value. Just as ancient pagans would rally around their gods, today's society rallies around personal identity markers—each person seen as a unique idol to be worshipped and defended at all costs.

This focus on personal identity, however, creates division, just as pagan practices often did. By elevating one group's identity over another, identity politics creates a society that is fractured and disconnected. It promotes a view of the world where individualism supersedes the common good, and community is sacrificed on the altar of self-definition.

In conclusion, the key ideologies of wokeism, techno-paganism, and identity politics are modern incarnations of ancient pagan beliefs. These movements, though seemingly progressive, have deep spiritual roots in self-worship, idolatry, and the rejection of divine truth. As the Church faces these threats, it is crucial to recognize that the battle is not only about societal norms but about defending the very heart of our faith and standing firm against spiritual darkness. By understanding these ideologies' connections to pagan thought, we can better equip ourselves to resist and stand strong in our call to defend the truth of God's Word.

Chapter 4: Strengthening the Church for the Battle

As the Church faces rising tides of pagan ideologies and spiritual decay, its strength lies not in buildings, programs, or political influence, but in its **spiritual resilience**. This resilience is built on a firm foundation of **sound doctrine, biblical education**, and **faithful discipleship**. To stand against the current cultural onslaught, the Church must be spiritually equipped and unified, prepared to engage in spiritual warfare with **prayer, scripture**, and a strong sense of community.

Spiritual Resilience Through Sound Doctrine and Biblical Education

The first and most crucial defense against modern-day pagan threats is **sound doctrine**. The foundation of the Church is its beliefs, and without a strong grasp of biblical truth, the Church will struggle to stand firm. As the Apostle Paul warns in **Ephesians 4:14,** believers should not be *"tossed back and forth by the waves, and blown here and there by every wind of teaching."* For the Church to withstand the pressures of today's secular ideologies, Christians must be equipped with an unshakable knowledge of God's Word.

Biblical literacy must be a priority in today's Church. In **Acts 2:42,** the early Church devoted itself to the teachings of the apostles. This commitment to studying and applying Scripture formed the foundation of the early Christian community. Likewise, modern Christians must move beyond surface-level understanding. We must be **biblically literate** to face the cultural storms ahead. Knowledge alone is not enough—it is crucial to **understand why we believe** what we do, so we can discern the difference between truth and lies.

In today's culture, where relativism is the norm and truth is seen as subjective, the Church's teaching must stand as an anchor of **absolute truth**. Without this solid foundation, Christians will be vulnerable to the rising tide of ideologies that challenge the unchanging truth of God's Word. To combat these shifting ideologies, we must hold fast to the foundational truths of Scripture—His holiness, His love, and His redemptive work through Christ. These truths must be firmly planted in every believer's heart, equipping them to stand firm against the tide of cultural and moral compromise.

Discipleship as a Foundation for Resisting Cultural Pressures

Sound doctrine alone is not sufficient to withstand the forces of cultural pressure. The Church must also prioritize **discipleship**—a dynamic, transformative process that equips believers to live out their faith in practical ways. Discipleship is not just about acquiring knowledge; it's about **application**—learning how to think biblically about the world and its challenges.

In Matthew 28:19-20, Jesus commands His followers to make disciples and teach them to obey His commands. Discipleship is both about **spiritual formation** and **cultural engagement**. In a world increasingly hostile to Christianity, discipleship must equip believers to navigate the cultural ideologies of today, including woke culture, identity politics, and the deification of technology. How can Christians engage with these ideologies without compromising their faith?

A **robust discipleship model** does more than teach doctrine; it builds **community**. The Church should be a place where believers can support each other in their journey to spiritual maturity. Discipleship must focus on **practical holiness**, teaching Christians to live out biblical principles in their personal lives, relationships, and engagement with the world. This includes everything from how believers spend their time and resources to how they respond to injustice and engage in public life.

Discipleship also requires **accountability**—teaching believers how to resist the tide of falsehoods and compromises that are gaining traction in society. When discipleship is rooted in the truth of Scripture and supported by a vibrant community, it becomes a powerful defense against cultural pressure.

Training Believers to Engage in Spiritual Warfare, Rooted in Prayer, Scripture, and Community

The rising pagan ideologies demand that the Church be prepared for **spiritual** warfare. Ephesians 6:12 reminds us that our battle is not against flesh and blood but against **spiritual forces of evil**. In these times, the Church must stand firm, not in its own strength, but in the power of God.

Prayer is our primary weapon in spiritual warfare. We must teach believers to **pray fervently**, seeking God's guidance and interceding for their communities and nations. Prayer strengthens the believer's faith and renews their commitment to standing firm. It is through prayer that we confront the spiritual forces behind the ideologies seeking to erode our values and faith.

In addition to prayer, **scripture** is a vital tool in spiritual warfare. It is the **sword of the Spirit**—our weapon against the lies of the enemy. Christians must prioritize regular **Bible study**, ensuring that the Word is not only known but deeply **internalized**. By memorizing and meditating on Scripture, believers are empowered to stand against deception and uphold the truth in the face of cultural pressures.

Lastly, **community** is essential in spiritual warfare. The Church is not a collection of isolated individuals; it is the **body of Christ**, called to support and encourage one another in the battle. Ecclesiastes 4:9-10 tells us, "Two are better than one... if either of them falls down, one can help the other up." The strength of the Church lies in its unity, as believers come together to support each other in prayer, accountability, and mutual encouragement.

The Church's strength to face the pagan uprising comes not from external factors but from its **spiritual resilience**. By focusing on **sound doctrine, discipleship**, and **spiritual warfare**, the Church can stand firm against the rising tide of secular ideologies and cultural pressure. **Biblical truth** must be deeply embedded in every believer's heart, **discipleship** must be more than academic but transformative, and the **community** must be united in prayer and action.

As we move forward, let us strengthen the Church with a renewed commitment to

God's Word, prayer, and **community**. Only then can we be prepared to withstand the pagan ideologies that seek to undermine the faith, and we will thrive as a **beacon of truth, hope**, and **transformation** in a dark world.

Chapter 5: A Call to Action: Defending Faith and Liberty

The time for passive observation is over.

The Church stands at a crossroads, facing an urgent call to action. The rise of pagan ideologies, secularism, and cultural movements that challenge Christianity has escalated to a point where inaction is no longer an option. We are called to not only resist these forces but to actively defend the faith, preserve liberty, and engage the culture around us. This chapter provides a practical guide for cultural engagement, offering strategic steps for Christians to take in order to defend their beliefs in the face of a world that increasingly rejects them.

A Practical Guide for Cultural Engagement and Standing Firm

In a culture where truth is often relative, Christians are called to stand firm in the unchanging Word of God. But standing firm does not mean retreating into isolation or remaining silent in the face of overwhelming opposition. Rather, it means engaging the culture with confidence, courage, and clarity. Cultural engagement begins with understanding the nature of the battle and the spiritual forces behind it.

The first step in cultural engagement is recognizing that Christianity is not merely a private faith but one that speaks into every area of life—from politics and education to art and entertainment. Christians are not meant to live in a bubble, detached from the world around them. **Matthew 5:13-16** calls us to be salt and light, offering preserving influence and guiding truth to a world in darkness. Cultural engagement involves understanding the issues at hand, discerning how they conflict with biblical principles, and taking strategic action to make a difference.

One of the most powerful ways we can engage with culture is by living out our beliefs in everyday life. This means making decisions, large and small, that reflect biblical values. Whether in the workplace, in the public square, or in personal relationships, Christians must be intentional about their witness. Each action, word, and choice is an opportunity to engage culture and bear witness to the truth of the Gospel.

But engagement is not passive. It requires courage. When we speak the truth in love, we will undoubtedly face resistance. But the Bible is clear: God has not given us a spirit of fear, but of power, love, and a sound mind *(2 Timothy 1:7)*. Standing firm in our beliefs does not mean hostility or confrontation, but it does mean speaking out with conviction and clarity, even when it's uncomfortable. Cultural engagement is rooted in love for others, but it is not afraid to challenge the lies that are so deeply embedded in the culture.

Strategic Steps for Christians to Resist Secularism and Counter Pagan Ideologies in Everyday Life

1. Equip Yourself with Knowledge of the Truth

A key step in engaging with culture is becoming biblically literate. Without a deep knowledge of Scripture, it's easy to be swept away by the shifting tides of cultural trends. 2 Timothy 3:16-17 reminds us that "All Scripture is God-breathed and is useful for teaching, rebuking, correcting and training in righteousness, so that the servant of God may be thoroughly equipped for every good work." Christians must become students of the Word, continually learning how it applies to modern life and the issues we face in the world.

2. Stand for Biblical Morality in Personal and Public Life

The battle for faith and liberty is not confined to public debates or political arenas—it begins in the home, the workplace, and the church. Christians must live out their beliefs daily, modeling biblical morality in all areas of life. This includes making ethical choices that honor God, practicing integrity, and serving others with love. Standing firm in biblical morality often means swimming against the current, but it is through our actions and choices that we demonstrate the reality of the Gospel in a world that is lost and searching.

3. Engage in Public Conversations with Confidence and Grace

Secularism, pagan ideologies, and moral relativism dominate much of the public discourse today. Christians are called to engage with these ideologies, not in anger, but in truth and grace. 1 Peter 3:15 commands us to "always be prepared to give an answer to everyone who asks you to give the reason for the hope that you have. But do this with gentleness and respect." When engaging with people in the public square—whether in conversation, on social media, or in the political realm—Christians must respond with humility, respect, and clarity.

4. Get Involved in Politics and Advocacy for Biblical Values

The public square is increasingly being shaped by secular and pagan ideologies. Christians must not shy away from political engagement and advocacy for issues that align with biblical values. This can include advocating for religious freedom, sanctity of life, traditional marriage, and freedom of conscience. While we are ultimately citizens of God's Kingdom, we are also citizens of this world and must engage politically to protect our liberties and influence society for good.

5. Support Christian Organizations and Movements that Defend the Faith

One of the most effective ways to defend faith and liberty is by supporting organizations that are on the front lines of this battle. Christian legal organizations, ministries, and advocacy groups like Alliance Defending Freedom, The Family Research Council, and The Heritage Foundation are all working to defend religious liberty and promote biblical values in the public sphere. Christians should support these organizations financially, through prayer, and by volunteering their time and talents to these causes.

How to Support the Public Defense of Christianity and Freedom

As Christians, we are not only called to defend the faith in our personal lives but to stand for it publicly. This requires active involvement in the cultural conversation—engaging with policymakers, participating in protests for moral causes, and supporting laws and policies that protect religious freedom. The defense of Christianity is a battle that happens both in the heart and in the public sphere.

It's crucial that Christians become public advocates for the faith—speaking up when religious liberty is threatened and supporting legislation that ensures the freedom to worship and live according to Christian principles. As the pagan uprising intensifies, Christians must make their voices heard, calling for policies that align with biblical truth, from the sanctity of life to freedom of speech.

Furthermore, Christians should support each other in this battle. Local churches, ministries, and individuals need to be unified in their mission to defend the faith. Just as soldiers in battle rely on one another for strength, Christians must lean on one another for encouragement, accountability, and support as they face opposition in their daily lives.

In conclusion, defending the faith and liberty in today's world requires active engagement, strategic action, and spiritual resilience. Christians must stand firm in their beliefs, counter pagan ideologies, and defend religious freedom in every sphere of life. The Church's role in this battle is not passive. We are called to take action, to live boldly, and to defend the truth—both personally and publicly. The stakes are high, but with a strong commitment to God's Word and a clear call to action, the Church can make a lasting impact in defending Christianity and liberty.

Chapter 6: Reclaiming the Public Square for Christ

In the early days of Christianity, the Church was not confined to the walls of a building or the quiet corners of society. It was a vibrant, public force, boldly proclaiming the Gospel and shaping the world around it. The Apostle Paul carried the message of Christ into cities, marketplaces, courts, and even the highest seats of power in the Roman Empire. Jesus Himself engaged with the public, challenging the religious leaders of His time and reshaping the moral fabric of society. However, over time, the Church has gradually retreated from the public square, allowing secular ideologies and pagan beliefs to fill the void. The cultural influence once wielded by Christians has been replaced by the growing tide of moral relativism, secularism, and paganism.

But this is not the end of the story. Reclaiming the public square for Christ is not only possible,it is essential. As society becomes increasingly hostile to biblical truths, Christians must rise up and take their rightful place in public discourse, restoring biblical values as the foundation for societal transformation. In this chapter, we'll explore why it is crucial for Christians to reclaim cultural influence, how leaders can engage in politics and media, and how the Church can reshape societal values in ways that honor God.

The Importance of Reclaiming Cultural Influence and Re-establishing Christian Values in the Public Sphere

Christianity has had a profound impact on Western civilization. From the abolition of slavery to the advancement of civil rights, the founding of universities, the development of social services, and the protection of human dignity, Christian principles have shaped the moral framework of society. But over the past century, there has been a noticeable shift—a move away from these foundational truths and toward secular and pagan worldviews that reject God's authority and moral order. As a result, the public square, once the arena for expressing biblical truth, has become a space where Christian values are marginalized or dismissed.

This shift is not inevitable, nor is it the end of the story. In **Matthew 5:13-16,** Jesus calls His followers to be the salt of the earth and the light of the world. Salt preserves and enhances, while light dispels darkness. In a world filled with moral decay and spiritual confusion, Christians are called to preserve and illuminate the truth. Reclaiming the public square for Christ means bringing biblical truth into every aspect of society politics, media, education, law, and culture.

The need for cultural engagement has never been more urgent. Christianity does not merely provide personal salvation; it offers a way of life—how to live in community, how to govern, and how to interact with others. The public square is where these principles are not only discussed but also applied. The absence of the Church in this space has left a void that has been filled by ideologies directly opposed to biblical truth. It is not enough to withdraw or remain silent. The Church must engage and transform the culture, offering a biblically grounded alternative to the secular worldview.

As the Apostle Paul writes in **Romans 12:2,** *"Do not conform to the pattern of this world, but be transformed by the renewing of your mind."* The Church is called to transform society, not by accepting its values but by challenging them and offering a biblical solution. This transformation begins with individual engagement but requires collective action from the Church as a unified body.

Actionable Steps for Christian Leaders to Engage in Politics, Media, and Cultural Movements

Christian leaders have a crucial role in leading the charge to reclaim the public square. With their unique platform, they have the power to shape culture, influence public opinion, and impact policy decisions. The Church is not merely a building; it is a community of believers equipped to take action.

Here are some actionable steps for Christian leaders to guide their congregations in engaging the public square:

1. Speak Boldly on Issues of Justice and Morality

Christian leaders must not shy away from cultural battles—from issues of justice, morality, and human dignity. The Bible speaks directly to issues like abortion, marriage, family, poverty, and racial justice.

These are not merely political talking points; they are moral imperatives that Christians are called to address through a biblical lens.

For example, in recent years, Christian leaders have played a significant role in advocating for the sanctity of life through movements like Pro-Life initiatives, where believers have rallied to protect the unborn. Similarly, in the battle for religious freedom, Christian leaders in the U.S. have stood strong, challenging policies that would silence Christian voices in the public sphere.

Leaders must speak out not just in church but in the public square, advocating for policies that align with God's Word. **Isaiah 1:17** calls believers to *"seek justice, encourage the oppressed, defend the cause of the fatherless, plead the case of the widow."* These words are as relevant today as when they were first spoken.

2. Equip the Congregation to Engage the Culture

Christian leaders cannot fight this battle alone. The entire Church must be prepared to engage culture and make a difference. This involves teaching biblical principles related to politics, morality, and societal issues. Leaders should offer biblical worldview training, civic education, and apologetics classes to help their congregation understand how to engage effectively with cultural and moral issues.

A great example of this engagement can be seen in the Christian Coalition in the U.S., which has worked to mobilize believers to vote according to biblical values. Similarly, many churches offer biblical citizenship courses to help members navigate political issues with a Christ-centered perspective.

3. Leverage Media and Technology to Spread the Gospel

The digital age has opened up vast opportunities to influence public opinion and shape the cultural narrative. Christian leaders should use media—whether through social media, podcasts, blogs, or television programs—to engage the culture and challenge the false narratives that are prevalent today.

One powerful example is The Benham Brothers, twin brothers who have used their platform to advocate for biblical values in business and media. Their success in media engagement has made them voices for Christian values in a secular culture.

Mark 16:15 tells us to *"go into all the world and preach the gospel to all creation."* The media provides Christians with the opportunity to fulfill this mandate and reach audiences who might never enter a church.

4. Engage in Political Advocacy and Legislation

The public square is increasingly being shaped by secular and pagan ideologies, and political advocacy is one of the most effective ways to reclaim it. Christian leaders must be involved in the political process, not just as voters but as advocates for biblical values. This can involve running for office, supporting godly candidates, or lobbying for policies that align with biblical principles, such as the sanctity of life and religious freedom.

A practical example of political advocacy is The Family Research Council, which works tirelessly to advocate for Christian values in Washington, D.C., influencing national legislation on issues like marriage and family.

How the Church Can Help Reshape Societal Values in a Biblically Grounded Way

The Church has a unique opportunity to reshape societal values by becoming an agent of transformation in the culture. Christians are called to demonstrate through their actions and words what a biblically grounded life looks like.

1. Live as a Counter-Cultural Community

The Church must model a way of living that is counter-cultural, reflecting biblical truths rather than the shifting sands of secular culture. This means promoting biblical family structures, upholding sexual purity, and valuing human dignity. Christians are called to live lives that are distinct from the world, offering a counter-narrative to the chaos and confusion that prevail in society.

Churches that emphasize family values and gender roles rooted in Scripture are making an impact in their communities. For example, Focus on the Family has worked for decades to champion the biblical understanding of marriage and family, impacting both individuals and lawmakers across the globe.

2. Advocate for the Common Good

The Church must also advocate for the common good, which includes promoting justice, freedom, and human rights. Christians must be active participants in societal conversations, addressing issues like economic inequality and social injustice with a biblical perspective.

The Church of the Nazarene, for instance, has been a key advocate for global human rights, particularly in areas like clean water, education, and poverty alleviation, all grounded in a Christian desire to serve the poor and oppressed.

3. Promote a Culture of Life and Hope

As secularism continues to grow, the Church must remain a beacon of hope, promoting a culture of life that values the sanctity of life from conception to natural death. The Church must actively resist movements like abortion and euthanasia while offering support and love to those facing difficult decisions.

Organizations like The 40 Days for Life Campaign and Crisis Pregnancy Centers exemplify the Church's role in supporting life in the public square. These ministries provide practical help for women in crisis pregnancies while advocating for pro-life policies.

Reclaiming the public square for Christ requires bold, intentional action in politics, media, and social movements. The Church must not retreat but step into the public arena, bringing biblical truth to bear on all areas of society. Through spiritual leadership, practical advocacy, and community engagement, Christians can reshape societal values and once again become a force that brings light to the darkness, truth to the lies, and hope to a world in desperate need of redemption.

By working together, the Church can transform culture, reclaim the public square, and honor God through a life of courage, conviction, and faithfulness.

Chapter 7: Preparing the Next Generation for the Battle

As the world drifts further from biblical truth, the next generation of believers faces an increasingly complex and hostile cultural landscape. Secular ideologies, pagan beliefs, and cultural movements challenge the core principles of Christianity, leaving young people at a critical crossroads. They must not only navigate these ideologies but stand firm in their faith and actively engage with the culture through biblical truth. This chapter focuses on equipping the next generation to defend the faith with courage and clarity.

Engaging Youth with Biblical Truth to Counteract Secular Ideologies

The battle for the minds of young people is well underway. Secular ideologies, like wokeism and relativism, permeate cultural discussions and tempt young believers with distorted views of justice, freedom, and personal identity. These ideologies offer an alternative to God's truth, promising progress and inclusion, but they often lead youth away from the solid foundation of biblical morality.

To counter these forces, it is vital to engage youth with biblical truth. This engagement is not just about teaching what young people believe but why they believe it. As 2 **Timothy 3:16-17** tells us, **"All Scripture is God-breathed and is useful for teaching, rebuking, correcting, and training in righteousness."** When youth understand the purpose and authority of Scripture, they gain the spiritual resilience to withstand the shifting ideologies that are taking over society.

For example, a church youth group in California recently launched a program aimed at addressing the increasing prevalence of woke culture in schools. By diving deep into biblical anthropology, they were able to counter the cultural narrative that undermines traditional Christian views on gender, human identity, and morality. Instead of simply opposing secular values, they focused on the biblical view of humanity, empowering youth to see themselves as God's image-bearers and understand their purpose within God's design.

The rise of techno-paganism and identity politics further exemplifies how secular ideologies have become ingrained in young people's lives. These movements place human autonomy and self-definition above divine order, which challenges the biblical truth that God alone defines human identity and moral purpose. By helping youth understand that truth is unchanging and rooted in God's Word, we equip them with the foundation needed to confront these ideologies head-on.

Mentorship, Apologetics, and Discipleship Programs for Younger Believers

Mentorship and discipleship are crucial for the next generation. Simply knowing the Bible is not enough; young people must apply biblical principles in real-life situations. The early Church understood this well—believers didn't learn in isolation. They were mentored by older, wiser believers who passed down faith and biblical wisdom.

In today's context, mentorship goes beyond teaching; it involves walking alongside youth as they engage with culture, offering practical wisdom for navigating secular pressures. One real-world example is the "True Love Waits" program, which encourages biblical views on sexuality through mentorship and personal accountability. This program empowers youth to stand firm in their commitment to sexual purity, countering the prevailing culture of promiscuity with teachings that emphasize God's design for marriage and family.

Similarly, apologetics programs must be integrated into discipleship. Apologetics equips young believers with the ability to defend their faith with clarity and conviction, especially when faced with cultural questions that challenge biblical truth. For instance, in high schools across the nation, Christian youth are regularly exposed to questions about evolution, moral relativism, and the existence of God. Providing them with apologetics training helps them respond with biblically grounded answers rather than retreating into silence.

A powerful example of apologetics at work is the Ravi Zacharias International Ministries (RZIM), which has hosted events where high school and college students could ask tough questions about their faith. By integrating apologetics into youth programs, the Church prepares young people to engage confidently with the counterfeit ideologies they face daily.

Discipleship programs must also emphasize spiritual formation. True discipleship is about transformation, not just education. It involves helping young people cultivate a deep, personal relationship with God, where their faith becomes the guiding principle in every aspect of life—from how they treat others to how they respond to social issues. These programs should teach youth that their identity and moral compass are rooted in biblical truth, not the shifting tides of cultural norms.

Empowering the Next Generation to Defend the Faith

Preparing the next generation is not just about providing them with knowledge. It is about empowering them to stand firm in their faith and engage a culture that increasingly rejects biblical values. This empowerment starts with spiritual formation, where youth learn to understand their identity in Christ and develop biblical convictions that guide their decisions.

Ephesians 6:10-11 encourages us to *"put on the full armor of God, so that you can take your stand against the devil's schemes."* Young people must be spiritually equipped to engage in spiritual warfare. This includes understanding that their battle is not against flesh and blood but against spiritual forces that seek to undermine God's truth in their lives. Spiritual warfare isn't just about resisting external influences; it's about standing firm in their personal relationship with God, understanding the role of Scripture, and knowing that the Holy Spirit empowers them for the journey.

We must also challenge youth to take ownership of their faith. This means not just going through the motions of belief but learning how to critically engage with the world around them. They must be able to articulate their beliefs, recognizing the tension between biblical truth and secular ideologies, and have the courage to speak out. A key example of this is the YouVersion Bible App, which offers a global community of young believers who can share thoughts on the Bible and engage in conversations about how faith applies to their daily lives.

Encouraging youth to take ownership of their faith also means giving them tools for engagement—not just in religious debates, but in practical social issues. For instance, how do they navigate conversations about sexual ethics, gender identity, or social justice in their school or university? Discipleship programs should give them a framework for answering these questions, based on biblical truth, while also teaching them to engage others with compassion and respect.

The Role of Community in Empowering the Next Generation

The Church community is one of the greatest assets in preparing the next generation. As **Hebrews 10:24-25** says, *"Let us consider how we may spur one another on toward love and good deeds... not giving up meeting together, as some are in the habit of doing, but encouraging one another."* The Christian community provides the support and accountability that youth need to thrive in their faith.

The importance of community is especially crucial in an age when youth face increasing pressure to conform to secular ideologies. When young people are supported by their peers in the faith, they gain the strength to resist pressure and stand firm in their beliefs. Programs like youth retreats, mission trips, and small groups can offer young people opportunities to grow spiritually in community, offering practical training and accountability as they learn to navigate a challenging world.

Real-life examples such as youth groups at Redeemer Presbyterian Church in New York, where young believers meet regularly to discuss cultural issues, help young Christians to be more equipped and bold in defending their faith. These programs help create spaces where youth can wrestle with difficult questions in a safe environment, which strengthens their spiritual resilience.

Preparing the next generation to defend the faith requires a holistic approach that combines biblical truth, mentorship, apologetics, and discipleship. Empowering youth involves helping them develop a personal relationship with God while teaching them to stand firm in the face of cultural ideologies. As the pagan ideologies of today continue to grow, the Church must rise to equip youth with the tools they need to stand strong. Spiritual formation, biblical literacy, and practical engagement with society will ensure that the next generation is ready to face the challenges ahead.

The future of the Church depends on the strength and spiritual resilience of its young believers. We must invest in their spiritual growth, equip them to defend their faith, and empower them to engage with the culture in ways that reflect the love, truth, and justice of Christ. Together, we can ensure that the next generation is ready to boldly declare the truth of the Gospel and stand firm against the rising tide of secularism.

Chapter 8: The Road Ahead: What the Church Must Do Now

The Church has always existed in tension with the surrounding culture. From the days of the Roman Empire to the rise of secularism in the modern world, Christians have had to choose whether they will stand firm on biblical truth or bend to the pressures of the age. Today, the pressure manifests in the form of a pagan threat;a godless uprising that seeks to redefine morality, reject divine authority, and replace Christianity with a culture centered on human autonomy, identity, and self-worship. The question before us is profound: What must the Church do now to defend the faith and liberty entrusted to it?

The answer is clear, but it requires courage: renewal, revival, and unity. To reclaim the culture and withstand the rising pagan threat, the Church must embrace a path of spiritual renewal, strengthen itself both locally and globally, and commit to collective action rooted in faith and biblical conviction.

Renewal and Revival as the Key to Reclaiming the Culture

Historically, when the Church faced overwhelming cultural and ideological opposition, renewal and revival have been the turning points. The Protestant Reformation, the Great Awakenings, and countless smaller revivals across the globe show that God's people can reclaim influence when they humble themselves, repent, and return to God's Word. The pagan threat today is not just political or social—it is fundamentally spiritual. Therefore, the solution must begin in the hearts of believers, leading to a spiritual awakening that equips the Church to stand firm.

Revival is not about emotional experiences or events. True revival is about the Holy Spirit awakening the Church to its mission, revitalizing hearts, and renewing commitment to biblical truth. It begins with repentance—recognizing where the Church has compromised with culture and turning back to God's Word. As **2 Chronicles 7:14** reminds us, *"If my people, who are called by my name, will humble themselves and pray and seek my face and turn from their wicked ways, then I will hear from heaven, and I will forgive their sin and will heal their land."*

Revival has the power to bring light into the growing darkness of our culture. A revived Church will regain its influence because it will reflect the holiness, love, and truth of Christ. When the Church is revived, it becomes a beacon of hope that transforms society. Consider how the revival movements in Eastern Europe led by the underground church were key in resisting communist oppression and eventually contributing to the fall of the Berlin Wall. The Church's strength, even in the darkest times, was its unwavering commitment to biblical truth—a commitment that shined through in both word and action.

In a time when pagan ideologies dominate politics, education, and entertainment, the only way forward is through a revived Church that lives differently, shines brightly, and speaks boldly.

Strengthening the Global Church to Withstand Rising Challenges

While revival begins in the hearts of individuals, the challenges facing the Church today are global. Pagan ideologies are not limited to America; they are spreading worldwide through media, technology, and cultural exchange. Secular humanism, radical inclusivity, and techno-paganism are influencing young people across Africa, Asia, Europe, and Latin America. The pagan threat is a global uprising against God's authority, and the global Church must be strengthened to meet these challenges.

A powerful example of global Christian unity can be found in The Lausanne Movement, which brings together church leaders from across the world to strategize and collaborate in evangelism and cultural engagement. By investing in biblical education, theological training, and leadership development for pastors and leaders worldwide, the Church can resist the spread of pagan ideologies and empower its leaders to stand firm against secular pressures.

1 Corinthians 12:14 reminds us that *"the body is not made up of one part but of many."* The global Church is one body, made up of countless congregations worldwide. To withstand the pagan threat, we must recognize our place within this larger family and collaborate across borders. Churches must share resources, pray for one another, and encourage each other in the faith. For example, when persecution is severe in places like China or North Korea,

Christians can rally in prayer, support through material aid, and share strategies for faithful endurance.

However, strengthening the global Church also requires confronting the false teachings creeping in under the influence of modern pagan ideologies. In parts of the world where secularism is on the rise, the Church must renew its commitment to Scripture as the final authority. When the Church compromises biblical truth for the sake of cultural relevance, it becomes vulnerable to division and confusion.

The Role of Christian Unity and Collective Action in Defending the Faith

No single congregation, denomination, or ministry can confront the pagan threat alone. The challenges are too vast, and the cultural forces too entrenched. To defend the faith and preserve liberty, Christians must commit to unity and collective action.

This does not mean ignoring differences in non-essential matters but rallying around the essentials of the faith—the authority of Scripture, the lordship of Christ, and the mission of the Church.

Jesus prayed in **John 17:21,** *"that all of them may be one, Father, just as you are in me and I am in you."* Unity brings strength, and division weakens our witness. When believers work together across denominations and traditions to defend the truth, the world takes notice.

In practice, this means partnering with Christian organizations and other denominations to advocate for biblical values in the public square. One of the most successful examples of this is The Christian Coalition in the U.S., which has helped unite Christians to advocate for pro-life policies, religious liberty, and moral values. Collective action also includes supporting those on the front lines of cultural engagement—whether Christian lawyers defending religious freedom, teachers shaping young minds, or artists bringing truth into the world of entertainment.

Collective action extends to spiritual warfare as well. When believers unite in prayer, they unleash spiritual power that can break strongholds and push back the darkness. As Ephesians 6:18 commands, "pray in the Spirit on all occasions with all kinds of prayers and requests... always keep on praying for all the Lord's people." Prayer must be the backbone of our collective action. Without it, our efforts are hollow. With it, we are empowered by God's power.

A Call to the Church Today

The pagan threat is real, and it is growing. But the Church has faced challenges before, and with God's help, it has always prevailed. The road ahead will not be easy, but it is filled with opportunity. Through renewal and revival, by strengthening the global Church, and by embracing unity and collective action, we can reclaim the public square for Christ and preserve both faith and liberty for generations to come.

The time to act is now. The Church cannot wait for another generation to take up this fight. It must rise today, with courage, conviction, and unwavering faith in the One who has already overcome the world. **Matthew 16:18** reminds us, *"I will build my church, and the gates of Hades will not overcome it."* The pagan threat may seem overwhelming, but the Church, strengthened by Christ, will stand.

Conclusion: The Final Stand—Faith, Liberty, and the Church's Future

Throughout history, every generation of believers has faced its own defining battle. For the early Christians, it was the Roman Empire's demands for loyalty to Caesar above Christ. For the Reformers, it was the corruption of truth within the very walls of the Church. For believers under oppressive regimes, it was the heavy hand of governments that outlawed faith and silenced truth. Today, the defining battle is the pagan threat—a godless uprising that seeks to remove Christianity from the center of culture and rewrite the moral fabric of society itself.

This battle is not only political, but spiritual. The pagan threat today is cloaked in the language of progress, inclusion, and justice, yet its core is rooted in idolatry and human autonomy—the elevation of the self above the Creator. It manifests in woke ideology, where identity is placed over truth, in techno-paganism, where human autonomy and technology are worshipped, and in identity politics, where the self becomes the highest point of devotion. These are modern forms of paganism, where created things are exalted above the Creator. As Lucas Miles warns in The Pagan Threat, this is not a distant concern, but a present reality. The Church can no longer afford to remain silent.

The final stand of the Church will determine its future. Will we retreat into the shadows, protecting only ourselves as the culture crumbles? Or will we rise to the challenge, reclaiming faith and liberty with courage and conviction? The future of the Church—and of nations shaped by its witness—depends on the answer we give today.

Faith: Anchoring the Church in Eternal Truth

At the heart of this battle is faith. Faith is not just a private belief—it is trust in God's unchanging Word, and the conviction that His truth is the standard for all of life. This kind of faith anchors the Church in the face of shifting cultural tides. It empowers us to stand when society pressures us to bow. As **Joshua 24:15** declares, *"As for me and my household, we will serve the Lord."*

The pagan threat seeks to erode faith by replacing it with doubt, distraction, and deception. Secular ideologies insist that truth is relative, that morality is subjective, and that faith is outdated. Yet, the Church must hold fast to the faith. **Hebrews 11:1** defines faith as *"confidence in what we hope for and assurance about what we do not see."* This faith is not fragile; it is a shield that protects us from the fiery arrows of the enemy. To secure the future of the Church, we must cultivate deep, unshakable faith—one that is boldly lived out in both public and private life.

Real-World Example: The Pro-Life Movement is a contemporary example of Christians standing firm in their faith. The Church's unwavering commitment to the sanctity of life—regardless of societal pressures—has led to the establishment of countless crisis pregnancy centers and pro-life advocacy groups. Through faith in God's truth, Christians continue to challenge the pervasive culture of death, showing the world that life is sacred from conception to natural death.

Liberty: Preserving the Freedom to Live and Proclaim the Truth

Faith and liberty are inseparably linked. Without liberty, faith becomes restricted to private spaces, losing its influence in the public square. Liberty allows us to worship freely, speak truth boldly, and live according to conscience without fear of reprisal. However, the pagan threat does not merely seek to silence faith; it aims to redefine liberty itself. Instead of liberty grounded in God's design, we see a counterfeit—freedom without boundaries, autonomy without accountability, and choice without truth. This false liberty does not lead to flourishing, but to chaos.

True liberty, as understood by the Founders of America, flows from God. As **2 Corinthians 3:17** reminds us, *"Where the Spirit of the Lord is, there is freedom."* Liberty is not the absence of restraint but the presence of God's Spirit, guiding us to live as we were created to live. If the Church abandons the defense of liberty, we will lose the freedom to proclaim Christ openly, to discipline the next generation, and to shape society according to God's truth.

Real-World Example: The Christian legal advocacy group Alliance Defending Freedom (ADF) has been instrumental in defending religious freedom in courtrooms across the U.S. ADF works to protect the freedom of Christians to speak and act in line with their beliefs in a culture increasingly hostile to biblical values. Their work serves as a model for how Christians can actively protect liberty for future generations.

The Church's Future: A Call to Courage and Unity

The road ahead is not easy. The pagan threat is growing stronger, evident in schools where children are taught to question God's design, in media where immorality is normalized, and in laws that attempt to silence biblical convictions. Yet, the Church has faced impossible odds before. We have the promise of Christ Himself: "I will build my church, and the gates of Hades will not overcome it" (**Matthew 16:18**). The Church's future is not one of defeat but of victory—if we remain faithful.

Courage is required. Courage to stand in the face of ridicule. Courage to speak truth when it is unpopular. Courage to live counterculturally when the cost is high. This courage does not come from ourselves; it comes from the Spirit of God working within us. **Acts 4:31** tells us that after the disciples prayed, *"they were all filled with the Holy Spirit and spoke the word of God boldly."* This same Spirit empowers us today.

The Church's future also requires unity. Division weakens the body of Christ, but unity multiplies its strength. The pagan threat thrives when the Church is fractured, but it falters when believers unite around the essentials of the faith. Denominational differences will not matter in the face of a cultural uprising that seeks to erase Christianity altogether. What will matter is whether we stand shoulder to shoulder, proclaiming Christ as Lord and refusing to compromise on truth.

Real-World Example: The Christian churches in Eastern Europe, particularly in Poland and Hungary, have shown remarkable unity in their defense of biblical family values and religious freedom. Despite opposition from secular European Union leaders, these churches have remained steadfast, finding strength in unity and shared commitment to God's

Word. Their collective stand has become a model for how the Church can resist political and cultural pressures with courage and unity.

A Final Stand

The final stand of the Church is not about reclaiming cultural dominance; it is about reclaiming faithfulness. It is about ensuring that, in every generation, the light of Christ continues to shine brightly in a dark world. The pagan threat is real, but it is not ultimate. The ultimate reality is Christ, seated at the right hand of the Father, reigning with power and authority over all things. Our task is to remain faithful until He returns.

The Church's final stand must be marked by three commitments:

1. Unwavering faith in God's Word
2. Steadfast defense of liberty
3. Courageous unity in the mission of Christ

If we hold to these, we will not only survive the pagan threat—we will overcome it. The culture may rage, governments may legislate against us, and false ideologies may spread like wildfire, but the truth of the Gospel will endure. As Jesus promised in **John 8:32**, *"Then you will know the truth, and the truth will set you free."*

The road ahead is clear. The Church must rise, not in fear but in faith, not in silence but in bold proclamation, not in isolation but in unity. The pagan threat is the defining challenge of our time, but it is also the defining opportunity.

Will we shrink back, or will we step forward? Will we compromise, or will we stand firm?

The choice belongs to us, but the outcome belongs to God.

The final stand is before us. May the Church choose faith. May the Church defend liberty. And may the Church's future be one of victory in Christ. **AMEN**